Jane Bauza

MW01596735

Bill Baumen
Asheville NC

Sacred Symbols From the

Avatars

Copyright © 2011 Mary and Barry Nadler

All rights reserved. This book may not be reproduced in whole or in part, or transmitted in any form, or by any means electronic, mechanical, photocopying, recording, or other, without written permission from the publisher.

ISBN-13: 978-0615549071

An avatar is a pure being; his pure body, visible as a light image, is free from any debt to nature.

On occasion, this God-man or God-woman casts no shadow nor makes any footprint on the ground. These are outward symbolic proofs of an inward freedom. Such a being knows the truth of Life and death.

Throughout the ages avatars have appeared in every walk of life, in every religion, race and nationality.

The Sanskrit word Avatar means "descent". In the Hindu scriptures, avatar signifies the descent of Divinity into flesh.

Dedication

We dedicate this book to Christ, Buddha, Maha Avatar Babaji, and all the great Avatars that assist the evolution of mankind. We thank God and the Great Ones for their love, guidance and blessings.

Our hope is that through the blessings, activations and initiations that are woven so powerfully and beautifully into the symbols and words in this book, you will come to know yourself as a light filled, love filled, masterful, powerful presence of God.

FORWARD

WE ARE ENGAGED IN CREATING VEHICLES OF HIGHER VIBRATION, THROUGH BOOKS, SEMINARS, PRAYER CIRCLES AND OTHER AVENUES, TO MANIFEST THE LIGHT QUOTIENT NEEDED ON OUR EARTH FOR ALL OF MANKIND'S ENLIGHTENMENT.

WITH GREAT LOVE AND RESPECT WE HONOR AND RECOGNIZE THE COMMITMENT OF OUR 20 PLUS FRIENDS WHO HAVE OVER SEVERAL MONTHS RECEIVED THE BLESSINGS, ACTIVATIONS AND INITIATIONS IN THIS BOOK AND WROTE THEIR TESTIMONIALS. ALSO, WE THANK OUR DEAR FRIEND PAUL GORDON FOR ALL OF HIS EFFORTS IN EDITING THIS BOOK.

WHILE YOU READ THIS BOOK YOU WILL RECEIVE THE BLESSINGS AND ACTIVATIONS FROM THE AVATARS TO FURTHER YOUR WHOLENESS IN ONENESS WITH THE PRESENCE OF GOD, THE SOURCE OF ALL LIFE. AS YOU MEDITATE ON THE SACRED SYMBOLS, WE KNOW THAT YOU WILL BE BLESSED ENORMOUSLY.

WE FEEL THAT THIS BOOK IS AN ESSENTIAL TOOL FOR SOUL EVOLUTION, AND THAT THE USE OF THESE SYMBOLS AIDS ONE IN ATTAINING SELF-MASTERY.

AS ALL OF US CONTINUE TO SPREAD THE LIGHT AND LOVE EXPONENTIALLY THROUGH MANKIND'S CONSCIOUSNESS, WE WILL REACH THAT TIPPING POINT WHERE THERE IS MORE LOVE THAN FEAR ON OUR DEAR PLANET. EVERYONE WILL AWAKEN TO THE PRESENCE OF GOD. WHEN THIS HAPPENS, A NEW ERA WILL BE BORN.

Preface

This book is the result of a process that began when the sacred symbols appeared to us in the summer of 2011. The symbols came into our conscious awareness with an onrush of powerful blessings which permeated the atmosphere of our inner world and outer experience.

When we received the symbols in this book, at first we did not know what they represented. It has been a delight to learn the history and power of these symbols that we received in pure innocence.

The accompanying activations and initiations created enormous shifts in our consciousness. The blessings that the symbols brought forth completed our awareness to create wholeness in the oneness of life that we continually experience.

Under the guidance of the avatars, we gathered a group of friends who over months would receive the blessings, activations and initiations to further their evolution. Our dear friends wrote the testimonials which are included in this book.

WE ARE SO THANKFUL THAT WE WERE INVITED TO RECEIVE AND DISTRIBUTE THE BLESSINGS OF THE SACRED SYMBOLS TO ALL THAT ARE INTERESTED. FOR US, BRINGING THESE SACRED SYMBOLS DOWN FROM THE HIGHER DIMENSIONS INTO THE EARTH PLANE, FROM THE HEART OF GOD INTO THE HEARTS OF MANKIND, HAS BEEN A MAGNIFICENT LIFE CHANGING EXPERIENCE.

Contents

God Portal to Higher Consciousness .. 15

Illuminated Love 21

God Peace 25

The Magic of Life 29

Harmony, serenity & Equanimity 33

Physical Healing 39

Psychological Healing 43

emotional Healing 47

Past Life Healing 51

Tree of Life 55

Soul Discernment 59

Relief from Human Tragedies 63

Truth and Purity 67

Unification of Divine Feminine and
Divine Masculine 71

Personal God Power 75

Beauty 79

Divine Grace, Abundance and
Prosperity 83

11

Freedom/Liberation from Ego 89

Wholeness in Oneness 95

Grand Unification 99

Christ Consciousness 103

Appendix — About the Authors 107

INSTRUCTIONS

Each symbol is an infinite vibration that activates and releases your own unlimited abilities and gifts to you.

We ask that before you begin each of your activations of the Sacred Symbols please do the following.

Sit quietly, become aware of your breath, center yourself, and allow your awareness to rest in your physical body and on your breathing.

Take several long, slow, deep, belly breaths and then return to normal breathing.

Feel the earth under you and the sky above you.

Now, allow your awareness to float to the top of your head...continue to float above your head 3 feet...now 6 feet...12 feet...going above the building that you are in, go above the forest, and continue to float above the earth, going to the higher dimensions of your Soul and spirit, bridging heaven and earth.

Allow your Soul to effortlessly move your conscious awareness upward, as if a loving invisible force is lifting you and unifying you with the higher dimensions while you continue to be sweetly grounded in your body on the earth.

YOU ARE BECOMING A DIVINE CONDUIT BRIDGING HEAVEN AND EARTH.

AS YOU BECOME A PERFECT CONDUIT FOR THE BLESSINGS FROM YOUR SOUL, THE HIGHER DIMENSIONS AND THE AVATARS, CONTINUE TO ALLOW LIGHT, LOVE, WISDOM AND POWER TO POUR DOWN, IN, THROUGH AND AROUND YOU ANCHORING IN AT THE BOTTOM OF YOUR SPINE. THE LIGHT OF GOD FLOWS DOWN THROUGH YOUR ARMS AND HANDS, LEGS AND FEET.

ALLOW THE LIGHT, LOVE, WISDOM AND POWER OF THE LIGHT OF THE EARTH TO FLOW UP THROUGH YOUR PHYSICAL BODY, MOVING UPWARD THROUGH THE BOTTOM OF YOUR FEET, LEGS, BASE OF YOUR SPINE, THEN CONTINUING UP YOUR SPINE, THROUGH YOUR ARMS AND HANDS AND OUT THROUGH THE TOP OF YOUR HEAD.

THE LIGHT OF THE EARTH AND THE LIGHT OF THE HEAVENS UNIFIES IN YOU.

YOU HAVE CREATED A PERMANENT BRIDGE OF LIGHT TO THE HEAVENLY DIMENSIONS AND TO YOUR PHYSICAL WORLD.

NOW, YOU ARE READY TO BEGIN YOUR ACTIVATIONS AND INITIATIONS WITH THE SACRED SYMBOLS FROM THE AVATARS.

God Portal to Higher Consciousness

The spiral is one of the most ancient symbols. A Golden Spiral represents the perfect plan of creation.

Meditation on Symbol

Visualize this golden spiral in your mind's eye.

Allow the activation to begin by remembering to relax and put your awareness on your breath.

Take several deep slow breaths from your abdomen.

As you visualize the symbol in your mind's eye you begin the blessing. You are now receiving an opening to the higher dimensions. This opening to the God portal, your God Presence, is a direct connection for you to the higher dimensions where the Great Ones reside, which allows continual blessings into you, your world, your business, your relationships and affairs.

This blessing and activation uplifts your human nature into your divine nature.

Feel the blessing flow down from above into your physical body; this infinite light and wisdom comes down through this portal which opens you to a higher consciousness.

This blessing activates the presence of God within you while creating a permanent divine bridge to your soul, spirit and the higher dimensions.

This infinite intelligence flows down into the top of your head, down through your body, anchoring at the base of your spine. This divine energy spreads throughout your entire physical body into your cells, organs and glands to uplift you.

We suggest you meditate on a symbol daily for 10-15 minutes. Visualize the symbol and then relax and allow the activations and blessings to flow through you.

Higher Consciousness

This gateway is to a higher consciousness which will assist you in expressing all the great and good things of God in your daily life.

You will unify more fully with your Soul and develop a soul consciousness allowing you to live a life that is more masterful, happier and fulfilled.

Mystics throughout the ages have written songs and poems about this unification. With these blessings there will be no longing for "a divine other". In oneness consciousness you realize you are the Divine Other, that God is within your breath, living the cells of your body, thinking the thoughts of the mind and expressing through your feelings. The illusion of separation from God drops away.

The illuminating light that pours through you from this magnificent God portal graces you with so many blessings. Relax and feel the grace and power of the blessing that you are receiving.

When you turn your attention to the God of us all, you feel the onrush of that power which comes from these heights of pure consciousness, surging into your feeling world and then into your awareness and consciousness.

These higher dimensions are permeated with a divine consciousness which will now flow down into you. This is where Christ, Buddha, The Angelic Kingdom, Ascended Masters, Avatars, Logos, Cosmic and Galactic Beings reside. They await your call to serve life. These Great Ones have gone before us to clear the way for our evolution.

All that is needed is an open heart, the inspiration to be of a higher consciousness, and to visualize the symbol; this opens the God Portal. After some time, a permanent unification is created to bridge heaven and earth.

The rushing of energy through the God Portal creates an awareness that you are ready to bless, heal, illuminate and prosper all.

You are becoming a radiating center for the most high. The opening to and access of this greater divine universe allows you to be a pure conduit of blessings for the universal good of mankind.

It is our experience that direct transmission of the pure light of God into the consciousness of one who is suffering, transforms them quickly and completely, and is much more efficient than going through years of attempting to sort out a problem using the human nature.

Our goal is to create a healthier and happier world by working in unison with the great ones to bless mankind with the highest vibration to create a pure collected consciousness of mankind.

We hope you join us in this endeavor!

Rest for a little while in communion with life in these higher dimensions and feel the unity that this activation creates.

Visualize the symbol daily, the more you utilize this blessing the more powerful it becomes.

Testimonial

"This portal, when opened, gives you a direct channel to the pure love energy of God. The more you open it the more powerful it becomes and the more connected you will feel to the God of which you are a part. This is not something you have to be good enough to access or have to earn. It is a gift of Grace that is pure Divine love waiting for you."

Hank Pierson
Black Mountain, North Carolina

19

Illuminated Love

The sacred symbol of a Golden Heart represents the unity of becoming one with divine love, and awakening to be Self-Realized through knowing that you are one with God through divine love.

Meditation on Symbol

Visualize the golden heart in your mind's eye.

Allow the activation to begin by relaxing and putting your awareness on your breath.

Take several deep slow breaths from your abdomen.

FEEL THE BLESSING OF ILLUMINATED LOVE, ENLIGHTENED LOVE, PURE LOVE FLOW DOWN FROM THE GOD PORTAL INTO YOUR PHYSICAL BODY, DOWN INTO THE TOP OF YOUR HEAD, DOWN THROUGH YOUR BODY AND ANCHORING AT THE BASE OF YOUR SPINE.

ILLUMINATED LOVE SPREADS THROUGHOUT YOUR ENTIRE BEING AND INTO YOUR PHYSICAL BODY, INTO YOUR CELLS, ORGANS AND GLANDS.

ATTUNE YOUR AWARENESS TO YOUR PHYSICAL BODY, AND FEEL WHERE THIS ACTIVATION IS TAKING PLACE WITHIN YOU AS WELL AS ABOVE YOU IN THE HIGHER DIMENSIONS.

WE SUGGEST YOU MEDITATE ON A SYMBOL DAILY FOR 10-15 MINUTES. VISUALIZE THE SYMBOL AND THEN RELAX AND ALLOW THE ACTIVATIONS AND BLESSINGS TO FLOW THROUGH YOU.

ILLUMINATED LOVE

THIS BLESSING CREATES ILLUMINATED LOVE, SELF LOVE, AND DEVOTION WITHIN YOUR HEART AND CONSCIOUSNESS. THIS VIBRATION IS THE LOVE OF AND FOR GOD.

THIS ACTIVATION ASSISTS YOU IN REMEMBERING YOUR LOVE AND CONNECTION WITH THE SUPREME POWER, THE ONENESS OF ALL LIFE.

AND FOR THOSE WHO MAY NOT FEEL WORTHY OF GOD'S GOOD AND GREAT GIFTS, THIS SYMBOL ALLOWS YOU TO ENTER INTO THE KINGDOM OF SELF LOVE.

WITH THE USE OF THIS SYMBOL YOU WILL FEEL THE BLESSING OF DIVINE LOVE INSIDE YOU. YOUR THOUGHTS, FEELINGS, AND ACTIONS BECOME MORE HARMONIOUS.

EACH OF US IS A CELL OF GOD IN THIS WORLD OF 7 BILLION CELLS OF GOD. IMAGINE OUR WORLD WHERE EVERYONE IS CREATING THE FEELING OF LOVE IN EVERY MOMENT.

PERHAPS YOU MAY TAKE A MOMENT, TAKE A BREATH AND ALLOW THIS THOUGHT AND FEELING IN.

WHEN YOU DO THIS YOU UNIFY WITH THE OTHER CELLS THAT ARE FEELING AND RADIATING ILLUMINATED LOVE, AND THE RESULT IS CREATING A UNIFIED FIELD OF ILLUMINATED LOVE IN THROUGH AND AROUND THE EARTH. TAKE A MOMENT EACH DAY AND FEEL THIS LOVE.

AFTER SOME TIME IN THE USE OF THIS BEAUTIFUL SYMBOL, YOU WILL NOTICE THAT THE PRESENCE OF GOD WITHIN YOU HAS GROWN STRONGER THAN THE EGO PERSONALITY. THIS IS A TIPPING POINT IN CONSCIOUSNESS WITHIN YOU THAT ALLOWS YOUR EXPRESSION IN LIFE TO BECOME MASTERFUL.

ILLUMINATED LOVE IS CHANGELESS AND CONSTANT. IT IS THE HIGHEST EXPRESSION AND THE ONE VIRTUE OF THE NATURE OF THE DIVINE, OF GOD. IN TIME, ILLUMINATED LOVE WILL BE THE HIGHEST EXPRESSION OF MAN.

A BEAUTIFUL QUOTE WE CHERISH IS, "BECOME CENTERED IN THE THOUGHT THAT TO MANIFEST DIVINE LOVE IS ALL THERE IS WORTH STRIVING FOR."

Testimonials

"The Symbol for Illuminated Love is to me the most beautiful one. When you activate any of the other Symbols with Love they are more powerful & more effective. I use this to create harmony with my beloved animals. I "beam" it out to them & it creates an energetic shift almost instantly. I also send it to any situation of discord whether it be personal or global. My biggest challenge is sending to myself but I am making progress.

I thank you Mary, Barry & the Great Ones for bringing these symbols to us."

Wendy Martin
Ypsilanti, Michigan

"Recently I have had the good fortune of working with Mary Nadler in an effort to transcend long standing personal issues which have created years of ill health and unhappiness. Feelings of separation from God and an inability to feel God's love topped the list. I walked through my days with an uncomfortable feeling there was something wrong needing to be fixed before I could love and accept myself unconditionally. Peace was the illusive dream.

Receiving the Sacred Symbols has been a profound experience there is no greater gift than the sublime moments of feeling God's presence in my heart. No longer feeling myself as flawed has allowed me to relax and enjoy my life and I'm relating to difficult people in situations in a more empowered fashion. I give thanks daily for these blessings and gifts responsible for my new found freedom."

Marcia Murphy
Asheville, North Carolina

24

God Peace

The Golden Circle of Peace is an ancient symbol of wholeness, of unity and the divine feminine.

Meditation on Symbol

Visualize the golden circle of peace in your mind's eye.

Allow the activation to begin by relaxing and putting your awareness on your breath.

Take several deep slow breaths from your abdomen.

Feel this blessing of Peace flow down through the God Portal into your physical body, down into the top of your head, down through your body and anchoring at the base of your spine.

This feeling of peace spreads throughout your entire physical body into your cells, organs and glands.

The blessing of Peace goes into your chakras, the crown, Throat, Heart, Solar Plexus, creative center and base of your spine. The golden circle of peace will float gently into every chakra, and that which is not peace is eliminated from you. You find within yourself a new strength and steadfastness that was not there before.

We suggest you meditate on a symbol daily for 10-15 minutes. Visualize the symbol and then relax and allow the activations and blessings to flow through you.

God Peace

In our daily life we strive to understand the behavior of ourselves and of our fellow brothers and sisters; the human and the divine within each of us. The life force within each of us is seeking to express our highest truth, our deepest knowing, the Love that we are. However, our experiences from the past can limit that expression of our divine selves.

By utilizing this symbol of peace we are more able to understand the depths of our beings and the behavior of others.

We are each a cell of God in this great Oneness of life. As we Master ourselves and become beings of Peace we resolve conflicts within ourselves and others.

By radiating the feeling of peace out into the atmosphere we encourage others in their ability to express in a loving and constructive manner. The essence of peace creates families, nations, and a global consciousness of peace.

Without question, when we feel peaceful everything is better!

Testimonial

"I sat with symbol #3 and here's what came up for me:
The soul often speaks without language—or rather, in a language other than words. Symbols hold the richness of the soul's gentle messages and allow us to connect—viscerally, deeply—to these blessings.

These messages are felt rather than heard, allowing for a far deeper experience than the interpretation of words allows—a deep knowing rather than a mere understanding.

When I contemplate the Golden Circle of Peace, I feel enveloped in a field of vibrant comfort— safe, supported, calm, protected and yet connected to all in an energizing way—and in that moment, I "know" peace.

THE ABILITY TO SUMMON AND FULLY EXPERIENCE THAT STATE INSTANTLY, AT ANY TIME IS THE PROFOUND GIFT OF THE GOLDEN CIRCLE OF PEACE."

R. PRUITT
SAN DIEGO, CALIFORNIA

Magic of Life

The Golden Five Pointed Star represents "the Star of Bethlehem" which assisted the Magi to find the Christ Child. We hope this sacred symbol will assist you in finding the magic of the Christ within you.

Meditation on Symbol

Visualize the golden five pointed star of the Magic of Life in your mind's eye.

Allow the activation to begin by relaxing and putting your awareness on your breath.

Take several deep slow breaths from your abdomen.

Feel this blessing of the Magic of Life flow down through the God Portal into your physical body, down into the top of your head, flowing down through your body and anchoring at the base of your spine.

This feeling of awe, of the Magic of God, spreads throughout your entire physical body into your cells, organs and glands.

We suggest you meditate on a symbol daily for 10-15 minutes. Visualize the symbol and then relax and allow the activations and blessings to flow through you.

Magic of Life

This activation creates a feeling of wonderment within you. You begin to realize how infinite God is, and how infinite you are.

The universe is full of mysteries and when we decide to go outside the box of conventional thought, we explore the possibilities in consciousnesses that are available to us.

By the use of this symbol of a golden five pointed star, we build a substantial feeling and awareness within us that life is a miracle.

Our lives change when we look through a new lens, a lens of The Magic of Life. We see The Magic of Life in nature, in a child's eyes, in our pets' movements and within the love that we share with each other.

Testimonial

"The Magic of Life, represented by a golden five-pointed star, is the perfection of God in Creation, the perfect synchronicity, the magic of all things as possible in God.

It is evident in the delight and wonder at seeing the Divine behind all things – it is the dance, the music, the artist's brushstroke, the lover's embrace – it is the perfect unfolding of everything-as-it-was-meant-to-be.

If we look with the eyes to see, and listen with the ears to hear, we see that God's magical Presence is there always, in all circumstances, in all beings, in our very selves.

"As we bring in this symbol, let us behold the radiant presence of God, that I Am Presence – let it enter the mind's eye and travel deep within the core of our consciousness, allowing it to radiate out to fill the physical body, the mental body, the emotional body, the etheric body – watching as it fills the room in which we find ourselves, our homes, our neighborhoods – extending out to our loved ones, embracing ALL as loved ones – extending out, out into the world and to all beings in this world and in all the worlds.

Let us abide in that joy, in that love, and in gratitude for this perfect moment."

Linda Gabby
Song of the Morning Ranch
Vanderbilt, Michigan

Harmony, Serenity and Equanimity

Cultures throughout history have used the Sacred Symbol of a Golden Flame. This symbol is to assist mankind in maintaining harmony and to represent the Sacred Fire of the Christ Flame.

Meditation on Symbol

Visualize a golden flame in your mind's eye.

Allow the activation to begin by relaxing and putting your awareness on your breath.

Take several deep slow breaths from your abdomen.

ATTUNE YOUR AWARENESS TO YOUR PHYSICAL BODY AND FEEL WHERE THIS ACTIVATION IS TAKING PLACE WITHIN YOU AND ABOVE YOU IN THE HIGHER DIMENSIONS.

ALLOW THIS FLAME, VIBRATION AND FREQUENCY TO EXPAND THROUGH YOUR BRAIN STRUCTURE, THROUGHOUT YOUR HEAD.

ALLOW THE GOLDEN LIGHT OF THIS FLAME TO PROCEED DOWN ALONG YOUR SPINE; ANCHORING THIS LIGHT AT THE BASE OF YOUR SPINE. NOW, CONTINUE TO EXPAND THE FLAME OUT INTO ALL OF YOUR BODIES (PHYSICAL, ETHERIC, EMOTIONAL, AND MENTAL...INCLUDING YOUR SUBCONSCIOUS MIND AND UNCONSCIOUS MIND).

THIS GOLDEN FLAME CONTINUES TO EXPAND UNTIL IT IS LARGER THAN YOUR PHYSICAL BODY. THE FLAME CREATES AN EXPANSION WITHIN YOU AND AROUND YOU OF THE FEELING OF HARMONY, SERENITY AND EQUANIMITY, EXPANDING OUT TO NINE FEET IN THROUGH, ABOVE AND AROUND YOU.

WE SUGGEST YOU MEDITATE ON A SYMBOL DAILY FOR 10-15 MINUTES. VISUALIZE THE SYMBOL AND THEN RELAX AND ALLOW THE ACTIVATIONS AND BLESSINGS TO FLOW THROUGH YOU.

HARMONY, SERENITY AND EQUANIMITY

AS YOU BUILD THIS ENERGY IN, THROUGH AND AROUND YOU, YOU CREATE A FORCE FIELD OF HARMONY, SERENITY AND EQUANIMITY. NOTHING IN THE OUTER WORLD CAN SHAKE YOU FROM THIS FEELING. THIS ASSISTS YOU IN CONSCIOUS MASTERY OF BALANCED ACTION.

IMAGINE A SHIP AT SEA IN A FEROCIOUS STORM AND A RESCUE HELICOPTER IS OVERHEAD ATTEMPTING TO DROP A LIFE LINE DOWN TO RESCUE THE OCCUPANTS OF THE SHIP. WHAT IF THE RESCUE TEAM IS UNABLE TO GET THE LIFELINE INTO THE SHIP BECAUSE THE TURBULENCE OF THE STORM AND SEA IS SO GREAT?

NOW SIMILARLY, IMAGINE SOMETHING HAPPENS TO YOU IN THE OUTER WORLD THAT CAUSES SUCH AN EMOTIONAL REACTION THAT YOU ARE UNABLE TO MAINTAIN ANY SEMBLANCE OF HARMONY. YOUR SOUL ABOVE YOU, IS THEN UNABLE TO BRING IN LIGHT FROM THE GODHEAD TO HARMONIZE YOUR FEELINGS. YOU WOULD BE IN A PLACE OF TURBULENT EMOTIONS THAT DESTROY YOUR WELL-BEING. ALSO, WHATEVER YOU ARE FEELING REGISTERS IN THE UNIFIED FIELD OF ALL LIFE.

WITH A POWERFUL FORCE FIELD OF HARMONY IN THROUGH AND AROUND YOU AND AN UNSHAKEABLE CONNECTION TO THE HIGHER DIMENSIONS, YOUR SOUL AND THE GODHEAD, YOU CAN MAINTAIN A STABLE FEELING OF HARMONY WITHIN YOU.

BY THE USE OF THESE SYMBOLS YOU BECOME A CONDUIT OF HEAVEN AND EARTH. YOU WILL FIND THAT BLESSINGS POUR INTO YOU AND OUT THROUGH YOU. YOU BECOME A RADIATOR OF THE HIGHEST DIVINE BLESSINGS. THIS SYMBOL OF HARMONY, SERENITY AND EQUANIMITY IS VERY IMPORTANT TO YOUR EVOLUTION. WHEN WE MASTER OUR FEELINGS AND STAY CALM THROUGH THE MOST DIFFICULT OF CIRCUMSTANCES, WE MOVE INTO SELF-MASTERY.

When we organize our thoughts in a harmonious manner and through divine love act in grace for the highest good of all, then we create a force field in, through, and around our bodies that is qualified with a vibration and frequency of our God Presence. These God qualities radiate the vibrations of harmony, serenity and equanimity into the world.

Testimonials

"When I sit with symbol #5 I feel this focused energy at my third eye and see a flame that is pink, purple and white. It expands so that it surrounds my body and the area around it. Then I feel a smaller flame moving thru my body and scrubbing in any areas where I have stuck energy."

K. L.
Asheville, North Carolina

"A golden flame in the center of my being expanded throughout the physical, auric and etheric bodies and rising to the heavens. Working with this symbol opens a pathway within our being that allows us to experience life in an increasingly calm and accepting way.

Equanimity, serenity and harmony that radiates through us also radiates out to the world, to everyone we meet and to all the circumstances we find ourselves in. This inner feeling of peace and surety helps to create harmony in our environment allowing divine love to spread throughout our entire area of influence.

THE INNER EMOTIONAL STABILITY AND SPIRITUAL WELL BEING THAT MANIFESTS CREATES A FOUNTAIN OF IDEAL VIBRATION IRONING OUT ANY DISHARMONY IT ENCOUNTERS, WITHIN AND WITHOUT.

THE MORE ONE WORKS WITH THIS SYMBOL THE MORE FAR REACHING THE EFFECTS AND THE GREATER THE CONTRIBUTION WE MAKE TO THE HARMONY OF THE WORLD. TRULY THIS IS A BLESSING OF CALMNESS AND STABILITY. EXPANSIVENESS AND ACCEPTANCE BLOSSOM AND FLOURISH. THE SPIRITUAL EYE BECOMES CLEARER AS INNER TURMOIL RECEDES AND THE CLOUDS OF DRAMA FADE AWAY. THANK YOU SO MUCH MASTERS BABAJI AND JESUS."

FRANK WHEELER
LONDON, ONTARIO

Physical Healing

This six sided yantra is empowered to activate your "inner healer".

The word yantra is a sanskrit word denoting a geometric design used for meditation and concentration. A yantra can be used as a visual mantra.

A yantra is a symbol of the highest spiritual and mystical powers. A yantra can be a cosmic conductor of infinite energy.

Meditation on Symbol

Visualize the golden symbol for physical healing in your mind's eye.

Allow the activation to begin by relaxing and putting your awareness on your breath.

Take several deep, slow breaths from your abdomen.

Attune your awareness to your physical body and feel where this activation is taking place within you and above you in the higher dimensions.

Invite this symbol of physical healing into the cells, organs and glands of your entire being. All the symbols have their own innate intelligence.

This symbol and blessing will go to wherever it is needed in your body, mind and soul.

When you visualize this symbol, surrender to the most high. Accept, allow and expect a great healing to occur.

We suggest you meditate on a symbol daily for 10-15 minutes. Visualize the symbol and then relax and allow the activations and blessings to flow through you.

PHYSICAL HEALING

The symbols in this book were designed by the Avatars to fulfill a specific purpose, as computer software is designed to fulfill a specific function.

INDIVIDUALLY AND COLLECTIVELY THESE SYMBOLS ARE DESIGNED TO INSPIRE AND MOVE MANKIND INTO A GREATER, MORE EXPANDED AWARENESS OF THE CHRIST CONSCIOUSNESS. THIS, IN TURN, CREATES A HEALTHY COLLECTIVE CONSCIOUSNESS. BY USING THESE SYMBOLS WE ARE CREATING A WORLD THAT IS KINDER AND MORE LOVING; A WORLD WHERE EVERYONE WILL EVENTUALLY BE ENGAGED IN EACH OTHER'S WELL-BEING.

MEDICAL SCIENCE AFFIRMS AND WE AGREE THAT PHYSICIANS AND TECHNOLOGY PROVIDE A HIGHLY VALUABLE SERVICE TO PROMOTE THE HEALING OF INDIVIDUALS.

THIS HAPPENS IN CONJUNCTION WITH THE INNER HEALER; THE INNATE DIVINE PRESENCE WITHIN YOU. THIS SYMBOL ACTIVATES YOUR INNER HEALER.

FOR US, UTILIZING THE RESOURCES AND GIFTS OF OUR DEAR GIFTED PHYSICIAN HAS ASSISTED US GREATLY AND SHE IS A BLESSING IN OUR LIVES.

WE ALSO SUBSCRIBE TO PREVENTIVE MAINTENANCE, SUCH AS EXERCISING, ACUPUNCTURE, HERBS, CHIROPRACTIC CARE AND MASSAGE TO MAINTAIN OUR EXCELLENT HEALTH.

EVERY PERSON ON OUR PLANET HAS THEIR OWN, INDIVIDUAL BLUEPRINT WITHIN THEIR SOUL AND I AM PRESENCE. WHEN THE DISCORD FROM THE PAST IS DISSOLVED FROM YOUR PHYSICAL, MENTAL, EMOTIONAL AND ETHERIC BODIES, THE RADIANCE OF YOUR DIVINE BLUEPRINT SHINES FORTH.

The sacred symbols assist in removing the discordant creations that are lodged within you. When removed, your inner consciousness reflects in your outer physical well-being, to create a life that is healthier, happier and more masterful.

In every moment of your life a miracle is taking place within you. Take a little time to become present to the miracle that you are. Take a breath and feel that your body is living! God is creating you in every moment.

Testimonial

"I am blessed to have received the #6 sacred symbol from the Avatars on physical healing. I use the symbol twice a day by picturing the golden circle with 6 strong triangles within it to clear all parts of my body including the blood, glands, organs, DNA, cells, bones, nerves, muscles, etc. The blessings keep giving to the oneness that we all are."

J. M.
Southport, North Carolina

Psychological Healing

The symbol of infinity represents that there is no beginning and no end, that we are all infinite and boundless by nature.

Meditation on Symbol

Visualize the golden symbol of infinity, a horizontal figure eight in your mind's eye.

Allow the activation to begin by relaxing and putting your awareness on your breath.

Take several deep slow breaths from your abdomen.

Attune your awareness to your physical body and feel where this activation is taking place within you and above you in the higher dimensions.

THIS SACRED SYMBOL COMES TO YOU FROM THE HIGHER DIMENSIONS TO BLESS YOUR WELL-BEING. THIS SYMBOL ACTIVATES THAT PERFECTION WHICH IS INNATELY WITHIN YOU TO CREATE BALANCE AND HARMONY WITHIN YOUR PSYCHE.

WE SUGGEST YOU MEDITATE ON A SYMBOL DAILY FOR 10-15 MINUTES. VISUALIZE THE SYMBOL AND THEN RELAX AND ALLOW THE ACTIVATIONS AND BLESSINGS TO FLOW THROUGH YOU.

PSYCHOLOGICAL HEALTH

BY THE USE OF THIS SYMBOL OF PSYCHOLOGICAL HEALING, ONE CREATES THE MASTER PRESENCE QUALITIES OF UNDERSTANDING AND INTELLIGENCE.

KNOW WITHIN YOUR HEART OF HEARTS THAT EVERYTHING THAT HAS HAPPENED TO YOU AND FOR YOU, HAD TO HAPPEN JUST THE WAY IT DID. IN THIS KNOWING THERE IS NO IMPERFECTION IN LIFE.

WITH THIS REALIZATION, THERE IS NO MOTIVE TO CONNECT WITH ANY NEGATIVITY SUCH AS JUDGMENT, LIMITING THOUGHTS, OR GOSSIP IN ANY WAY, SHAPE OR FORM.

WITH THIS EXPANDED CONSCIOUSNESS INTO THE HIGHER, DIVINE, ENLIGHTENED MIND AND THE HIGHER ASPECTS OF YOUR SELF, ONE FEELS THE ACCEPTANCE OF ONE'S DIVINITY.

When you know that your enlightened consciousness has become greater than your human nature, the tipping point in consciousness has occurred in the depths of your being. You feel yourself expressing from your divine consciousness rather than your human consciousness. This creates the greatest psychological well-being. You are free to create, play and fulfill your divine plan.

Testimonial

"The Truth of this symbol is that deep psychological healing comes from the knowing that we are boundless, immortal beings and that, in each one of us, is the potential for this realization and the experience of the bliss of this reality. Knowing this, we can also know that there really is no death and no separation between people, or between us and God, apart from that which we choose to see. Where there is no death and no delusion of separation, there is no need for fear, for anger, for despair, past, present, or future, or for any human vice that gives rise to fear, anger, or despair in others. That gives us the freedom to live authentic lives with integrity and courage and rid ourselves of the karma we have accumulated in the past lives we have lived in ignorance of this profound and compelling Truth. In understanding this symbol, we are offered relief, not from the vicissitudes of life, which help us to work through our karma, but from the suffering that we assume necessarily accompanies them."

Wendy L.
London, Ontario

Emotional healing

This healing vortex was brought to us by the Avatars for freedom from emotional blockages. This vortex is a powerful mass of energy that moves in a whirling motion seeking out and removing any obstacles in its way, to create a clear and calm emotional state.

Meditation on the Symbol

Visualize the golden vortex in your mind's eye.

Allow the activation to begin by relaxing and putting your awareness on your breath.

Take several deep slow breaths from your abdomen.

Attune your awareness to your physical form and feel where this activation is taking place within you and above you in the higher dimensions.

This symbol of a golden vortex drops down from the Avatars in the higher dimensions, into the center of your physical body and expands through your emotional body to dissolve old hurts, wounds and traumas.

It has been reported that sometimes as many as 10 golden vortexes appear in, through, and around an individual, depending on what their life experience has been.

We suggest you meditate on a symbol daily for 10-15 minutes. Visualize the symbol and then relax and allow the activations and blessings to flow through you.

emotional Health

In our beautiful schoolroom called earth, one of the reasons we are here is to achieve mastery in thought, word, deed, feeling and action.

To create harmony in feeling can be a true challenge for many individuals. The emotional body is the largest of all the four lower bodies and can be sent into an emotional whirlwind at the slightest provocation.

We have found that this symbol assists in creating a calm feeling within your self.

Not only does this sacred symbol release the past hurts and traumas, but also this symbol was "programmed" to activate your true consciousness.

In your true consciousness you aspire to be the full expression of your God Presence.

With your true consciousness you learn the law of harmlessness. You bring tranquility in all your interactions with life.

When you feel the subtle shadows of your lower bodies beginning to engage you, simply visualize the golden vortex to remove these feelings.

You will learn to walk gently upon our dear earth, and when in nature you will honor the beauty that has been created for your enjoyment.

You feel peaceful, content and alive in an ever-new way.

Whatever you feel is what you are directly adding to life, to God. Begin to fully live your life as a loving ritual to yourself, to others and to the I Am Presence.

As your heart is made to be a song of gratitude, know that you are one with all divinity as you express this feeling in your thoughts, speech and your actions.

Testimonial

"As we received the activation of the symbol for emotional healing I felt it more profoundly than any other one. When I "bring them in" for myself & my family each day, I still feel it very strongly. This tells me how much of my healing needs are emotional (this is not a surprise to me :-)) I am so grateful for their wonderful gifts. Thank you Mary, Barry & the Great Ones. "

Wendy Martin
Ypsilanti, Michigan

"I invoked symbol #1 The God Portal, then #8 Emotional Healing Symbol. Immediately I became aware of my injured right shoulder.

As the energy moved into the shoulder, I experienced emotional stresses regarding burdens within daily life releasing. Within my spiritual eye, I perceived a cellular repair process at the DNA level was occurring.

During this process I experienced a reduction in shoulder pain and a realignment of the shoulder joint and improved movement of my arm."

Carrie Bodane
Raleigh, NC

Past Life Healing

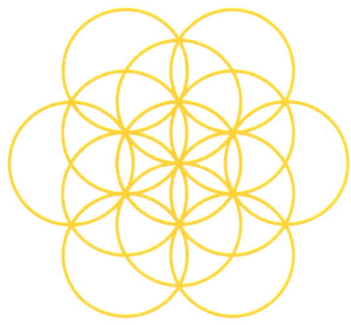

The Golden Flower of Life is a universal sacred symbol representing all-that-is.

Meditation on Symbol

Visualize the golden flower of life in your mind's eye.

Allow the activation to begin by relaxing and putting your awareness on your breath.

Take several deep slow breaths from your abdomen.

The Flower of Life is one of the oldest sacred symbols known to man. The Flower of Life can be found in churches, temples, art, and manuscripts of diverse cultures from around the world.

THE TEMPLE OF OSIRIS IN EGYPT, WHICH DATES BACK OVER 6,000 YEARS, CONTAINS THE OLDEST KNOWN EXAMPLES OF THE FLOWER OF LIFE.

ATTUNE YOUR AWARENESS TO YOUR PHYSICAL BODY AND FEEL WHERE THIS ACTIVATION IS TAKING PLACE WITHIN YOU AND ABOVE YOU IN THE HIGHER DIMENSIONS.

WE SUGGEST YOU MEDITATE ON A SYMBOL DAILY FOR 10-15 MINUTES. VISUALIZE THE SYMBOL AND THEN RELAX AND ALLOW THE ACTIVATIONS AND BLESSINGS TO FLOW THROUGH YOU.

PAST LIFE HEALING

THE FLOWER OF LIFE REPRESENTS THE VISUAL EXPRESSION OF THE CONNECTIONS OF ALL LIFE, INDIVIDUALLY, COLLECTIVELY, GLOBALLY AND UNIVERSALLY. WE ALL HAVE WOVEN OUR STREAM OF CONSCIOUSNESS THROUGH LIFE AND THROUGH ALL OF MANKIND.

OUR PAST IS RECORDED WITHIN WHAT ARE CALLED THE AKASHIC RECORDS OF ALL LIVING THINGS. THE AKASHIC AND THE FLOWER OF LIFE ARE INTERWOVEN IN A NON-PHYSICAL DIMENSION.

THIS SACRED SYMBOL IS DESIGNED TO CLEAN AND PURIFY WHATEVER YOU HAVE RECORDED THROUGHOUT YOUR LIFE STREAM THAT IS NOT THE PURITY OF THE CHRIST. THE USE OF THIS SYMBOL WILL CREATE A FRESH, NEW BEGINNING FOR YOU AND YOUR LIFE.

THE SACRED SYMBOLS ARE GREAT TOOLS OF MASTERY WHICH ASSIST WITH PHYSICAL, PSYCHOLOGICAL AND EMOTIONAL HEALING.

Once the mind understands and the heart experiences the clarity, peace, strength and stability within you, a new world emerges.

Testimonial

"This is an extraordinary power symbol. This symbol journeys throughout your stream of life and corrects your past interactions, perceived mistakes and discord of any and all kinds to create a life free from old unhelpful patterns and conditioning.

This is the main, the greatest symbol among all the sacred symbols. It is the most comprehensive healing symbol that covers all the different levels of bodies & planes from the beginning of time of existence as a human.

As it travels along the spine it changes sizes, shapes and the intensity of glow. It brings fullness & perfection in the lotus flower of that region and then finally turns into one gigantic, perfect flower that is good enough for the Creator."

H.K.
North Carolina

Tree of Life

The Tree of Life is a universal symbol found in many spiritual traditions around the world. This sacred symbol is used as a sign of unity and love and the unrestricted fullness of life. It is one of the most familiar and ubiquitous of the Sacred Geometry Symbols.

Meditation on Symbol

Visualize the golden tree of life in your mind's eye.

Allow the activation to begin by relaxing and putting your awareness on your breath.

Take several deep slow breaths from your abdomen.

Visualize the symbol in your mind's eye. See the golden branches going forth to the sun, sky and universe, "The Father", and the roots going into the earth, "The Mother".

Attune your awareness to your physical body form and feel where this activation is taking place within you and above you in the higher dimensions.

We suggest you meditate on a symbol daily for 10-15 minutes. Visualize the symbol and then relax and allow the activations and blessings to flow through you.

Tree of Life

This symbol clears your etheric body from all the history that you have created and accumulated in your journey since you left the heart of God.

The etheric body is one of the four lower bodies. It is another dimensional aspect of yourself that houses your divine plan.

If you feel that you are not expressing from your highest divine potential and your divine nature, it is because your blueprint, your God presence, is covered up by the effects of past actions.

The etheric body is susceptible to damage and weakening by mental stress, physical injury, surgeries, and other life traumas.
This symbol brings a profound initiation which cleanses and heals the etheric body.

IN THE MORNING WHEN YOU AWAKEN, AND IN THE EVENING AT BEDTIME, VISUALIZE THE GOLDEN TREE OF LIFE COMING UP THROUGH THE BOTTOMS OF YOUR FEET, ANKLES, CALVES, KNEES, THIGHS, HIPS, SOLAR PLEXUS, CHEST, SHOULDERS, ARMS, HANDS, NECK AND HEAD, ALL THE WAY UP THROUGH YOUR PHYSICAL BODY, AND THEN ALLOW THE BLESSING TO DO WHAT IT HAS BEEN DESIGNED TO DO.

NOTICE AND FEEL THE CUMULATIVE RESULTS IN THE MORNING WHEN YOU AWAKEN. EVEN AFTER ONE WEEK, FEEL THE LUMINOUS DIFFERENCE IN YOUR CONSCIOUSNESS THAT HAS MANIFESTED.

TESTIMONIALS

"WHEN YOU FIRST INTRODUCED THIS SACRED SYMBOL — GOLDEN VIBRANT TREE OF LIFE-TO US , I IMAGINED A GREAT BIG TREE WITH THE TOP BRANCHES REACHING UP INTO THE HEAVENS AND THE LONG STURDY TRUNK COMING DOWN TO THE WIDESPREAD ROOTS AND THOSE ROOTS REACHING DOWN INTO MOTHER EARTH! I THEN , FROM HOW YOU DESCRIBED IT TO US, SAW THE GREAT LIGHT FROM HEAVEN COMING DOWN INTO THE TOP OF THE TREE AND THE LOVING LIGHT FROM MOTHER EARTH COMING UP FROM THE ROOTS AND UP THE TRUNK TO MEET THE LIGHT FROM THE HEAVENS AND THEY JOIN AND LITTLE LIGHT BEINGS JOIN HANDS AND DANCE AROUND THE BIG LIGHT SHAFT JOINING HEAVEN & EARTH! I FEEL HAPPY WHEN I SEE THOSE LITTLE BEINGS DANCING MERRILY AROUND AND AROUND THE TRUNK BRINGING IN THAT JOYOUS JOINING OF HEAVEN & EARTH AND IN THAT JOY MY ETHERIC BODY IS BEING LOVING HEALED AND CLEANSED ! THANK YOU, THANK YOU, THANK YOU!"

ANN FROM MICHIGAN

"Each time I have sat with this symbol it changes or evolves. Today, the ends of the branches, rather than the fire I've seen so many times, were leaf shaped portals to other dimensional aspects of my etheric body. I went into each. There are different tones and dimensional aspects comprising each one. As things shift, the tones become more congruent. Then the differentiation of the leaf-like portals disappears, there is one chord, and the connection to the earth or a grounding energy intensifies, the flow becomes unified, and strong."

Carol Seaver
South Palm Beach, Florida

Soul Discernment

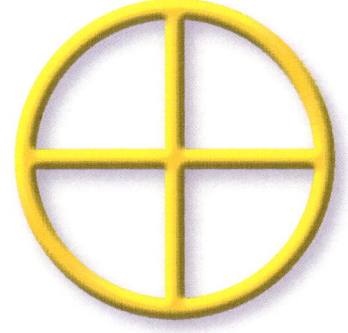

This ancient symbol of the solar cross marks the four seasons, the solar calendar for the ancients. For the Native Americans this symbol represents the four directions.

Meditation on Symbol

Visualize the golden circle with a cross in your mind's eye.

Allow the activation to begin by relaxing and putting your awareness on your breath.

Take several deep slow breaths from your abdomen.

Attune your awareness to your physical body and feel where this activation is taking place within you and above you in the higher dimensions.

As above, so below!

This symbol aligns one with the physical body and with your soul's wisdom and the higher aspects of your self. This allows for the highest divine discernment to be present at all times in your life.

We suggest you meditate on a symbol daily for 10-15 minutes. Visualize the symbol and then relax and allow the activations and blessings to flow through you.

Soul Discernment

One of the greatest gifts from our Souls and from God is the ability to discern what is the truth.

The Grace of being one with your Soul's wisdom and living your life from this inner, deep knowing, allows you to create a life that is one with your divine purpose.

In this Oneness you become a "tuning fork" for the wisdom of your soul, the truth of your being. You are able to put your life into action to create the harmony and love of a soul-centered life.

Testimonial

"I listen to the gift as it enters to hear its message, and I feel its vigorous and dynamic energy, enabling clear contact with my Soul.

My Soul actively, each moment, offers me the Truth, the I AM clarity of every condition and message I encounter.

This wonderful gift is more than a parting of the curtains to see the I AM of each moment. It is a pathway of the expression of the Truth.

Soul Discernment goes beyond processing or questioning to enable the consciousness of Being the I AM in every moment."

A.D.
Asheville, North Carolina

Relief from Human Tragedies

This eight spoke wheel is representative of the eight-spoke dharma wheel.

We have learned that soon after the Buddha achieved his enlightenment, Brahma came down from heaven and requested the Buddha to teach and offered him a symbol of the teachings, an eight spoke wheel, representing Buddha's doctrines.

Brahma's other message to Buddha that day was that whoever sets new teachings into motion, changes the course of destiny.

Meditation on Symbol

Visualize this golden wheel with 8 spokes in your mind's eye.

ALLOW THE ACTIVATION TO BEGIN BY REMEMBERING TO RELAX AND PUT YOUR AWARENESS ON YOUR BREATH.

TAKE SEVERAL DEEP SLOW BREATHS FROM YOUR ABDOMEN.

YOU WILL FEEL THE BLESSING FLOW FROM ABOVE YOUR PHYSICAL BODY, COMING DOWN FROM THE HEAVENS THROUGH YOUR OVER-SOUL AND SOUL, DOWN INTO THE TOP OF YOUR HEAD, DOWN THROUGH YOUR BODY AND ANCHORING AT THE BASE OF YOUR SPINE. THE ENERGY SPREADS THROUGHOUT YOUR ENTIRE PHYSICAL BODY INTO YOUR CELLS, ORGANS AND GLANDS.

AS THE LIGHT OF YOUR SOUL FLOWS DOWN FROM THE HEAVENS INTO YOUR PHYSICAL BODY, THERE IS AN OPENING TO THE HIGHER DIMENSIONS ABOVE YOUR HEAD.

THE ILLUMINATING LIGHT FROM GOD POURS THROUGH YOU AND GRACES YOU WITH SO MANY BLESSINGS.

THIS DIVINE LIGHT POURS INTO YOUR PHYSICAL BODY, MENTAL BODY, EMOTIONAL BODY AND ETHERIC BODY.

THE LIGHT OF GOD CONTINUES TO ANCHOR INTO YOU AT THE BASE OF YOUR SPINE, AND THEN DOWN INTO THE EARTH.

WE SUGGEST YOU MEDITATE ON A SYMBOL DAILY FOR 10-15 MINUTES. VISUALIZE THE SYMBOL AND THEN RELAX AND ALLOW THE ACTIVATIONS AND BLESSINGS TO FLOW THROUGH YOU.

Relief from Human Tragedies

Accept all the experiences you have had and are having in your life.

Allow yourself to experience the pain, anger, resentment, any and all lower vibrational feelings that have been stored from your life experience.

Allow these feelings to come to the surface. Go into a witnessing state of consciousness. Acknowledge your feelings. Put your awareness on the symbol.

Now, through divine alchemy, the lower vibrations from the tragedies become transformed into the truth of who you are, pure Love.

Visualize the symbol daily. The more you use this blessing the more real and powerful it becomes to you.

Testimonial

"Upon hearing this sacred symbol I had immediate sense of relief. And while contemplating the symbol during the follow-up blessing I strongly felt the words 'self doubt' well up from the core of my being and express themselves in my throat. It was a command to let go of my age old

SELF DOUBT (MY PERSONAL TRAGEDY). I KNOW THAT WHEN I DOUBT MYSELF I DOUBT MY POTENTIAL AND MY DIVINITY, SO THIS SYMBOL WAS A TRUE BLESSING FOR ME."

P.D.
ASHEVILLE, NC

Truth & Purity

The circle represents divinity and the pyramid within the circle represents the journey a soul takes upon departing from the heart of god. One side of the pyramid represents birth, another side represents the journey, and finally the third side represents becoming one with the ultimate truth and purity of the state of self-realization, a pure state of being.

Meditation on the Symbol

Visualize this golden pyramid in your mind's eye.

Allow the activation to begin by remembering to relax and put your awareness on your breath.

TAKE SEVERAL DEEP SLOW BREATHS FROM YOUR ABDOMEN.

YOU WILL FEEL THE BLESSING FLOW FROM ABOVE YOUR PHYSICAL BODY, COMING DOWN FROM THE HEAVENS THROUGH YOUR OVER-SOUL AND SOUL, DOWN INTO THE TOP OF YOUR HEAD, DOWN THROUGH YOUR BODY AND ANCHORING AT THE BASE OF YOUR SPINE. THE ENERGY SPREADS THROUGHOUT YOUR ENTIRE PHYSICAL BODY INTO YOUR CELLS, ORGANS AND GLANDS.

AS THE LIGHT OF YOUR SOUL FLOWS DOWN FROM THE HEAVENS INTO YOUR PHYSICAL BODY THERE IS AN OPENING TO THE HIGHER DIMENSIONS ABOVE YOUR HEAD.

THE ILLUMINATING LIGHT FROM GOD POURS THROUGH YOU AND GRACES YOU WITH SO MANY BLESSINGS.

THIS DIVINE LIGHT POURS INTO YOUR PHYSICAL BODY, MENTAL BODY, EMOTIONAL BODY AND ETHERIC BODY.

THE LIGHT OF GOD CONTINUES TO ANCHOR INTO YOU AT THE BASE OF YOUR SPINE, AND THEN DOWN INTO THE EARTH.

WE SUGGEST YOU MEDITATE ON A SYMBOL DAILY FOR 10-15 MINUTES. VISUALIZE THE SYMBOL AND THEN RELAX AND ALLOW THE ACTIVATIONS AND BLESSINGS TO FLOW THROUGH YOU.

Truth and Purity

This initiation into the higher truth & purity of all things is a turning point into greater self-mastery and ultimately into full mastery.

This initiation brings in clarity of mind that allows you to know when you perceive the truth in a thought, situation, or experience.

From this place of self-mastery, you will know the choice to make, or path to take, that leads you to do what is for your highest good. Actions taken in this way can only create positive, fulfilling outcomes in your life.

This symbol also brings the removal of self-doubt.

Visualize the symbol daily. the more you use this blessing the more real and powerful it becomes to you.

Testimonial

"My experience of this symbol is of a three dimensional, three sided pyramid of equilateral triangles- four sided including the base, slowly revolving inside a golden circle, which radiates a fiery energy, appearing like solar flares emanating from the surface of the sun.

Meditating deeper, I became aware, and could feel the subtler qualities and characteristics of this symbol, beyond the obvious qualities of truth and purity that it conveys. These qualities

69

ARE STRENGTH, DISCERNMENT, CLARITY, INCISIVENESS, STABILITY AND UNCOMPROMISING STEADFASTNESS.

BEING SOMEONE WHO 'FEELS' THE QUALITIES THAT DIFFERENT THREE DIMENSIONAL SHAPES EXPRESS, ITS INTERESTING HOW PERFECT THE TETRAHEDRAL PYRAMID IS FOR THIS SYMBOL, BEING AS IT IS, THE STRONGEST AND LEAST 'CORRUPTIBLE' STRUCTURAL FORM THERE IS IN THE PHYSICAL WORLD AS WELL."

PAUL GORDON
TORONTO, CANADA

Unification of Divine Feminine and Divine Masculine

This symbol represents the unity of the divine feminine and divine masculine. The initiation in this symbol creates a non-dualistic state of consciousness and awakens you to the reality that we are all one with each other and one in this vast cosmos.

This realization unfolds by the harmonizing of our characters and creating a foundation for masterful behavior in all endeavors.

Meditating on the Symbol

Visualize this golden yin/yang symbol in your mind's eye.

71

ALLOW THE ACTIVATION TO BEGIN BY REMEMBERING TO RELAX AND PUT YOUR AWARENESS ON YOUR BREATH.

TAKE SEVERAL DEEP SLOW BREATHS FROM YOUR ABDOMEN.

YOU WILL FEEL THE BLESSING FLOW FROM ABOVE YOUR PHYSICAL BODY, COMING DOWN FROM THE HEAVENS THROUGH YOUR OVER-SOUL AND SOUL, DOWN INTO THE TOP OF YOUR HEAD, DOWN THROUGH YOUR BODY AND ANCHORING AT THE BASE OF YOUR SPINE. THE ENERGY SPREADS THROUGHOUT YOUR ENTIRE PHYSICAL BODY INTO YOUR CELLS, ORGANS AND GLANDS.

AS THE LIGHT OF YOUR SOUL FLOWS DOWN FROM THE HEAVENS INTO YOUR PHYSICAL BODY THERE IS AN OPENING TO THE HIGHER DIMENSIONS ABOVE YOUR HEAD.

THE ILLUMINATING LIGHT FROM GOD POURS THROUGH YOU AND GRACES YOU WITH SO MANY BLESSINGS.

THIS DIVINE LIGHT POURS INTO YOUR PHYSICAL BODY, MENTAL BODY, EMOTIONAL BODY AND ETHERIC BODY.

THE LIGHT OF GOD CONTINUES TO ANCHOR INTO YOU AT THE BASE OF YOUR SPINE, AND DOWN INTO THE EARTH.

WE SUGGEST YOU MEDITATE ON A SYMBOL DAILY FOR 10-15 MINUTES. VISUALIZE THE SYMBOL AND THEN RELAX AND ALLOW THE ACTIVATIONS AND BLESSINGS TO FLOW THROUGH YOU.

Divine Feminine and Divine Masculine

Union with your divine feminine and divine masculine is to develop the pure, divine qualities of perfect feeling (feminine) and perfect reason (masculine).

Once this is accomplished, the feminine and the masculine become spiritually united and then one merges in God.

Imagine living your life in balance with your divine feminine and divine masculine natures. Become consciously aware of Oneness within you, creating a balanced, harmonious life.

This sacred symbol creates greater harmony in all your relationships, from the relationship you have with yourself, to the relationship you have with all life.

Visualize the symbol daily. The more you use this blessing the more real and powerful it becomes to you.

Testimonial

"THE DIVINE MASCULINE AND FEMININE EMBODY STRENGTH AND ENDURANCE. IN A FORWARD MOVEMENT WE EMBRACE TRUST, INTUITION, ACTION AND NURTURING. TO RESONATE WITH THESE VIBRATIONS WE BECOME AWARE OF THEIR PRESENCE AND FEEL A BALANCE OF THESE COMPLIMENTARY UNIVERSAL POWERS. THIS LEADS TO FULFILLMENT COMPLETE IN HARMONY WITH OURSELVES AND THOSE AROUND US - ESPECIALLY THOSE WHO ARE CLOSEST TO US IN OUR DAILY LIVES.."

ANDY BODANE
RALEIGH, NORTH CAROLINA

Personal God Power

The Golden Ocean represents the omnipresent, omniscient and omnipotent presence of life, of God. With the initiation of this symbol you expand out into the universe becoming one with every atom of cosmic consciousness. Your awareness continues to expand, expand and expand into the infinite oneness which is the ultimate reality of life.

Meditation on the Symbol

Visualize a golden ocean in your mind's eye.

Allow the activation to begin by remembering to relax and put your awareness on your breath.

Take several deep slow breaths from your abdomen.

You will feel the blessing flow from above your physical body, coming down from the heavens through your Over-Soul and Soul, down into the top of your head, down through your body and anchoring at the base of your spine. The energy spreads throughout your entire physical body into your cells, organs and glands.

As the light of your Soul flows down from the heavens into your physical body there is an opening to the higher dimensions above your head.

The illuminating light from God pours through you and graces you with so many blessings.

This divine light pours into your physical body, mental body, emotional body and etheric body.

The light of god continues to anchor into you at the base of your spine, and down into the earth.

We suggest you meditate on a symbol daily for 10-15 minutes. Visualize the symbol and then relax and allow the activations and blessings to flow through you.

Personal God Power

This initiation to unify your higher power with your personal divine power creates the exquisite refinement of true power. To own your power is a great step forward in self-mastery.

True power has nothing to do with force or the lower vibrations of human consciousness. True Power embodies an intellectual understanding of cosmic law as well as the ability to bless life with your sagely expression of living life from a place of knowing that you are the presence of God, the highest vibration, and you always seek an outcome of a "win win" situation for all. The wisdom of your Soul expresses through your intellect and feelings. The actions of the past no longer infiltrate your expression.

You develop a deep and profound ability to listen to a person, to nature, to life, and your interpretation comes from the level of Soul and Spirit. This can only lead you to the most comprehensive, loving outcome.

Visualize the symbol daily, the more you use this blessing, the more real and powerful it becomes to you.

Testimonial

"Symbols one thru four took us thru our personal healing and adjustment per our requirement. Symbol Fifteen is viewed as a graduation step at this point, where the perfection of creation is realized. The sacred nature of all life and structure both planetary and universal comes into alignment. We notice once again the mastery of this plan, its universal intelligence. In this sea of golden light we realize, once again oneness. We, our very oneness, is God."

Bill McC.
San Diego, California

BEAUTY

THE PEARL IS A WONDERFUL SYMBOL FOR THE PROCESS OF EVOLUTION. IT BEGINS WITH A GRAIN OF SAND, AND OVER TIME TRANSFORMS INTO AN OBJECT OF GREAT VALUE AND BEAUTY.

THE GOLDEN PEARL IS PERHAPS THE RAREST OF ALL NATURAL PEARLS IN OUR WORLD. IT IS SAID THAT THESE PEARLS HOLD THE INCANDESCENT RAYS OF THE SUN. THE GOLDEN PEARL REPRESENTS WEALTH, GOOD HEALTH, PROSPERITY AND GREAT BEAUTY.

IN THE BIBLE'S BOOK OF REVELATIONS, THE AUTHOR DESCRIBES PEARLS AT THE GATES OF HEAVEN.

MEDITATION ON THE SYMBOL

VISUALIZE THIS GOLDEN PEARL IN YOUR MIND'S EYE.

ALLOW THE ACTIVATION TO BEGIN BY REMEMBERING TO RELAX AND PUT YOUR AWARENESS ON YOUR BREATH.

TAKE SEVERAL DEEP SLOW BREATHS FROM YOUR ABDOMEN.

YOU WILL FEEL THE BLESSING FLOW FROM ABOVE INTO YOUR PHYSICAL BODY, COMING DOWN FROM THE HEAVENS THROUGH YOUR OVER-SOUL AND SOUL, DOWN INTO THE TOP OF YOUR HEAD, DOWN THROUGH YOUR BODY AND ANCHORING AT THE BASE OF YOUR SPINE. THE ENERGY SPREADS THROUGHOUT YOUR ENTIRE PHYSICAL BODY INTO YOUR CELLS, ORGANS AND GLANDS.

AS THE LIGHT OF YOUR SOUL FLOWS DOWN FROM THE HEAVENS INTO YOUR PHYSICAL BODY, THERE IS AN OPENING TO THE HIGHER DIMENSIONS ABOVE YOUR HEAD.

THE ILLUMINATING LIGHT FROM GOD POURS THROUGH YOU AND GRACES YOU WITH SO MANY BLESSINGS.

THIS DIVINE LIGHT POURS INTO YOUR PHYSICAL BODY, MENTAL BODY, EMOTIONAL BODY AND ETHERIC BODY.

THE LIGHT OF GOD CONTINUES TO ANCHOR INTO YOU AT THE BASE OF YOUR SPINE, AND DOWN INTO THE EARTH.

WE SUGGEST YOU MEDITATE ON A SYMBOL DAILY FOR 10-15 MINUTES. VISUALIZE THE SYMBOL AND THEN RELAX AND ALLOW THE ACTIVATIONS AND BLESSINGS TO FLOW THROUGH YOU.

Golden Pearl

This symbol restores a person's beauty in character, mind, heart and soul. This affects personal inner beauty and outer physical beauty.

This initiation into the pure beauty of who you are allows the human spirit to soar to the highest level and reflect your God nature to all life.

This is a powerful initiation into the truth of you. You will be able to express your life from the nature of your spirit.

Imagine creating beauty from the inner-most beautiful you. Beauty permeates the atmosphere of your life With every breath that you take. From your sphere of influence you exude beauty into every living thing on the earth.

You bring joy and loveliness wherever you go, by exalting the spirits of others through your presence.

Visualize the symbol daily, the more you use this blessing, the more real and powerful it becomes to you.

Testimonial

"Tonight after my evening meditation, I was going over in my mind some things that have been weighing heavily on me. I began to visualize the golden pearl and felt myself starting to smile. I had this peaceful feeling of love that I felt radiating out to the other people in the room with me. And I still feel that calming peace an hour later."

A.P.

Divine Grace, Abundance and Prosperity

This golden portal opens you to a higher level of energy that will assist you in creating true prosperity, and living in a universe of abundance and grace.

When we are in the "flow of our Souls", that inspiring feeling within us is what we call Grace. When things in our lives work out in a way that is harmonious, loving, with an outcome that feels good to us, this too we call grace.

The energy of grace is always with us and in all things. However, choices in our lives can make us feel that we are separate from grace. The truth is that grace permeates every atom in the universe.

With this golden portal to the higher dimensions and the blessing that can come to you when the portal is open, you will know and experience the three components of this initiation; divine grace, prosperity, and an unlimited abundance of all good and great things.

Meditation on the Symbol

Visualize this golden Portal in your mind's eye.

Allow the activation to begin by remembering to relax and put your awareness on your breath.

Take several deep slow breaths from your abdomen.

You will feel the blessing flow from above your physical body, coming down from the heavens through your Over-Soul and Soul, down into the top of your head, down through your body and anchoring at the base of your spine. The energy spreads throughout your entire physical body into your cells, organs and glands.

As the light of your Soul flows down from the heavens into your physical body there is an opening to the higher dimensions above your head.

The illuminating light from God pours through you and graces you with so many blessings.

THIS DIVINE LIGHT POURS INTO YOUR PHYSICAL BODY, MENTAL BODY, EMOTIONAL BODY AND ETHERIC BODY.

THE LIGHT OF GOD CONTINUES TO ANCHOR INTO YOU AT THE BASE OF YOUR SPINE, AND DOWN INTO THE EARTH.

WE SUGGEST YOU MEDITATE ON A SYMBOL DAILY FOR 10-15 MINUTES. VISUALIZE THE SYMBOL AND THEN RELAX AND ALLOW THE ACTIVATIONS AND BLESSINGS TO FLOW THROUGH YOU.

GOLDEN PORTAL

THIS INITIATION CREATES IN YOUR FEELINGS AND DEEP INNER KNOWING, THAT YOU HAVE AND ALWAYS WILL HAVE MORE THAN ENOUGH OF ALL THAT YOU NEED.

THE INITIATION OF GRACE IS TO SANCTIFY YOU, CREATING A STATE WHERE YOU SHARE IN A DIVINE LIFE FILLED WITH ABUNDANCE AND PROSPERITY.

WHEN YOU ARE FILLED WITH GRACE, ABUNDANCE AND PROSPERITY, YOU FEEL THAT YOUR SOUL IS BEAUTIFUL. THERE IS SPLENDOR IN YOUR COUNTENANCE. YOU FEEL ELEVATED INTO A MORE ENLIGHTENED MIND AND LIFE. YOUR ACTIONS BECOME MORE GRACE FILLED, CREATING GREATER OUTCOMES FOR A GRACE FILLED LIFE.

THE FEELING AND KNOWING OF BEING ONE WITH THE VIRTUES OF YOUR SOUL, INCLUDING GRACE, ABUNDANCE AND PROSPERITY, GIVES YOU AN INNER POWER TO EXPRESS YOUR HIGHEST DIVINE QUALITIES. YOU WILL ALWAYS CREATE THE HIGHEST OUTCOME FOR ALL, IN ANY GIVEN SITUATION, CIRCUMSTANCE OR RELATIONSHIP.

WITH THE FEELING AND REALITY OF HAVING MORE THAN ENOUGH OF WHATEVER YOU NEED, IT IS EASY TO BE GENEROUS, WHICH FULFILLS THE UNIVERSAL LAW OF THE CIRCLE. THAT WHICH WE RADIATE INTO COLLECTIVE LIFE RETURNS TO US MANIFOLD. THIS IS DIVINE GRACE IN ACTION.

THIS INITIATION ALSO ENABLES OUR MINDS TO SEE INTUITIVELY. WE ARE THEN ABLE TO ASCERTAIN THE HIGHEST TRUTH IN OUR LIVES AND THE LIVES OF OTHERS, IN ORDER TO SHARE OUR BLESSINGS WITH THEM.

TRULY EMBODYING GRACE, ABUNDANCE AND PROSPERITY, WE BECOME INSPIRED TO DRAW CLOSER TO OUR DIVINITY AND TO ALWAYS ACT FROM THE PLACE OF AN ENLIGHTENED CONSCIOUSNESS FOR THE HIGHEST GOOD OF ALL.

YOUR SPIRIT SOARS DUE TO THE INCREASED FEELING OF WELL BEING AND YOU BECOME ONE WITH YOUR GOD VIRTUES. BY DOING SO, YOU IN TURN EXALT OTHERS' FEELINGS INTO AN ENHANCED ONENESS WITH THEIR SOULS AND SPIRITS.

VISUALIZE THE SYMBOL DAILY. THE MORE YOU UTILIZE THIS BLESSING, THE MORE REAL AND POWERFUL IT BECOMES TO YOU.

TESTIMONIAL

"I see the symbol of a "spiral" start spinning at the base of my spine and traveling up the spine. I realized this is the "key" to the door, to the portal, the portal of Grace, Abundance & Prosperity. Once the key is unlocked & the door opened, I see myself standing inside - but there was no inside or outside since the door was not attached to any walls or rooms. It was standing by itself in the middle of nowhere, Infinite Universe."

H.K.
North Carolina

Freedom/Liberation from Ego

The Maltese Cross dates back to the 12th century and the First Crusade. This symbol was used by the Knights Templar, the Knights of Malta, and the Order of St. John of Jerusalem among others. Later this symbol became an award for acts of heroism, bravery and leadership skills.

Meditation on the Symbol

Visualize this Maltese Cross in your mind's eye.

Allow the activation to begin by remembering to relax and put your awareness on your breath.

Take several deep slow breaths from your abdomen.

You will feel the blessing flow from above your physical body, coming down from the heavens through your Over Soul and Soul, down into the top of your head, down through your body and anchoring at the base of your spine. The energy spreads throughout your entire physical body into your cells, organs and glands.

As the light of your Soul flows down from the heavens into your physical body there is an opening to the higher dimensions above your head.

The illuminating light from God pours through you and graces you with so many blessings.

This divine light pours into your physical body, mental body, emotional body and etheric body.

The light of god continues to anchor into you at the base of your spine, and down into the earth.

We suggest you meditate on a symbol daily for 10-15 minutes. Visualize the symbol and then relax and allow the activations and blessings to flow through you.

GOLDEN MALTESE CROSS

THIS INITIATION INTO FREEDOM IS LIBERATION FROM THE EGO PERSONALITY INTO A PERSONALITY THAT IS CHRISTED. YOU WILL EXPRESS MORE FROM YOUR GOD-VIRTUES IN EVERY THOUGHT, FEELING, SPOKEN WORD AND ACTION.

WHEN THE PRESENCE OF GOD BECOMES LARGER THAN YOUR HUMAN CONSCIOUSNESS, THE TIPPING POINT OCCURS. YOU CAN NOTICE THIS IN THE WAY YOU THINK, FEEL, WALK, TALK, AND INTERACT WITH PEOPLE, NATURE, FAMILY, FRIENDS AND LIFE.

ONE OF THE GREATEST HUMAN TRAGEDIES THAT CREATES AN UNHEALTHY WEB OF THINKING, IS THE NOTION OR FEELING THAT SOMETHING IS WRONG; EITHER WITH YOURSELF, OTHERS, THE WORLD, OR GOD.

IT IS POSSIBLE TO GET CAUGHT IN THESE LOOPS OF THINKING, SUCH AS "IF ONLY I WOULD HAVE DONE THAT DIFFERENTLY", OR "IF ONLY THEY WOULDN'T HAVE BETRAYED ME?", OR "WHY DO THEY LIE TO ME". THESE THOUGHTS AND EMOTIONS KEEP US STUCK IN THE HUMAN EGO AND IN THE LOWER DIMENSIONS.

WHEN SOMETHING INSIDE OF US WANTS DEARLY TO MOVE AWAY FROM ANGER, HATRED, REVENGE AND ALL THE LOWER EMOTIONS, AND WE DESIRE TO MOVE INTO FORGIVENESS OF OTHERS AND OURSELVES, IT IS THE FIRST STEP TO FREEDOM.

THE NEXT STEP TO FREEDOM IS TO EXPAND OUR CONSCIOUSNESS. USE OF THE MEDITATION DESCRIBED AT THE BEGINNING OF OUR BOOK TAKES YOU OUT OF HUMAN CONSCIOUSNESS INTO THE HIGHER DIMENSIONS WHERE ONLY GOD QUALITIES EXIST.

AS A RESULT, NEW THOUGHTS ENTER INTO CONSCIOUSNESS, THOUGHTS THAT ARE OUTSIDE OF THE BOX OF WHAT HAD BEEN "NORMAL" THINKING. IT IS INDEED DARING AT FIRST TO ALLOW OURSELVES TO THINK IN THIS NEW WAY.

LET US NOW ASK THE QUESTION:

WHAT IF YOU KNEW THAT EVERYTHING THAT HAS HAPPENED TO YOU HAD TO HAPPEN JUST THE WAY IT DID? IN FACT, THIS IS A GREAT TRUTH.

LET'S SAY IT AGAIN, TO EMPHASIZE THIS GREAT TRUTH:

EVERYTHING THAT HAS HAPPENED TO YOU AND IN THE WORLD AT LARGE HAD TO HAPPEN JUST THE WAY IT HAPPENED.

THIS TRUTH HAS BEEN DESCRIBED IN VARIOUS WAYS AS KARMA, PHYSICS—THE LAW OF CAUSE AND EFFECT, ONENESS, AND OTHER EXPRESSIONS THROUGHOUT DIFFERENT CULTURES.

LET THIS NEW WAY OF THINKING SINK IN COMPLETELY INTO YOUR CONSCIOUSNESS. ALLOW YOUR BODY TO LET THIS FLOW INTO YOUR AWARENESS.

JUST THINK OF A NEW LIFE FOR YOURSELF AND OTHERS WITHOUT BLAME, JUDGMENT, ANGER, SADNESS, GRIEF. ALLOW ALL THE QUALITIES OF YOUR HUMAN NATURE TO SHIFT INTO YOUR GOD QUALITIES OF LOVE, HAPPINESS, JOY, UNDERSTANDING, AND COMPASSION.

THIS IS FREEDOM.

WE ARE IN A NEW ERA WHERE HIGHER TRUTHS ARE DROPPING DOWN FROM THE HEAVENS LIKE GOLDEN RAIN. THERE IS A SHIFT IN CONSCIOUSNESS WITHIN ALL PEOPLE AROUND OUR BEAUTIFUL PLANET.

YOU CAN SEE IT IN THE COUNTRIES IN NORTHERN AFRICA, A PHENOMENON BEING CALLED THE "ARAB SPRING", WHERE DICTATORS WHO KEPT A NATION AND PEOPLE IN STRIFE, POVERTY AND REPRESSION ARE BEING OVERTHROWN.

IN THE UNITED STATES THERE ARE MOVEMENTS TO CHANGE THE WAY THINGS HAVE BEEN DONE IN THE PAST, TO NEW WAYS OF THINKING ABOUT HOW TO CREATE A SUCCESSFUL CULTURE. ALL SYSTEMS OF THE WORLD ARE BEING RE-EVALUATED AND EVENTUALLY WILL CHANGE FOR THE BETTER.

THE GREAT ONES, THE AVATARS, ARE POURING THEIR BLESSINGS INTO THE EARTH PLANE MOMENT TO MOMENT FOR EVERYONE.

EMBODY THE WISDOM OF YOUR SOUL AND EXPRESS FROM THIS NEW LEVEL OF CONSCIOUSNESS TO CREATE A BETTER LIFE FOR YOURSELF AND ALL.

VISUALIZE THE SYMBOL DAILY. THE MORE YOU UTILIZE THIS BLESSING THE MORE REAL AND POWERFUL IT BECOMES TO YOU.

Testimonial

"There really is a feeling of liberation, of being able to watch the drama unfold yet being able to keep one's peace as a result of concentrating on the Maltese Cross of Freedom. Understanding grows and along with it, patience naturally expresses itself. Trust increases which lessens the apparent "need" to try to plan the future to make it happen the way one wants it to instead of the way it needs to for one's highest good."

J.P.

Wholeness in Oneness

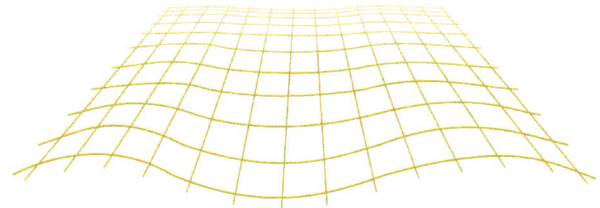

The spiritual meaning of the unified field is that when our consciousness of Oneness becomes more perfect, we discover our Oneness with all life and the feeling of unity becomes increasingly more apparent.

When we become aware of the universal truth that we are all one and we know ourselves as this one consciousness, this one Spirit, we create in this unified field a life that reflects that consciousness.

Beauty and love permeate our thoughts, feelings and actions. Happiness bubbles up inside us. Positive thoughts fill our consciousness and we are drawn to beauty, creativity and love. Peace becomes a living reality within our consciousness.

Meditation on the Symbol

Visualize this golden matrix in your mind's eye.

Allow the activation to begin by remembering to relax and put your awareness on your breath.

Take several deep slow breaths from your abdomen.

You will feel the blessing flow from above your physical body, coming down from the heavens through your Over-Soul and Soul, down into the top of your head, down through your body and anchoring at the base of your spine. The energy spreads throughout your entire physical body into your cells, organs and glands.

As the light of your Soul flows down from the heavens into your physical body there is an opening to the higher dimensions above your head.

The illuminating light from God pours through you and graces you with so many blessings.

This divine light pours into your physical body, mental body, emotional body and etheric body.

The light of god continues to anchor into you at the base of your spine, and down into the earth.

We suggest you meditate on a symbol daily for 10-15 minutes. Visualize the symbol and then relax and allow the activations and blessings to flow through you.

Unified field — golden matrix of light

This extraordinary symbol helps to bring together in a cohesive manner, all the activations, initiations and blessings that you have received.

To feel one with god can be fleeting. This symbol stabilizes the feeling of oneness and brings about the feeling of wholeness within you. This allows for a continuous feeling and endless experience of oneness with the vast universal self of which you are.

You know, that you know, that you know, that everything that has taken place in your life had to happen just the way it happened, and that this truth has brought you into freedom.

Calmness and peace are your natural state. Allow your new expansive state of consciousness to fill in places in yourself where human consciousness previously existed.

Allow yourself to become one in wholeness with the unified field.

VISUALIZE THE SYMBOL DAILY. THE MORE YOU UTILIZE THIS BLESSING THE MORE REAL AND POWERFUL IT BECOMES TO YOU.

TESTIMONIAL

"I AM ENGULFED IN AN EXPANSIVE GOLDEN SPACE. NONE OF THE BUSYNESS OF THE DAY IS THERE — IT IS INFINITELY SILENT YET VIBRANT WITH ENERGY. I AM THE ONLY OBJECT, AND THEN I DISSOLVE INTO THE PURE GOLDENNESS. I WONDER IF I CAN SEE COLORS, AND BEAUTIFUL COLORS APPEAR. I WONDER IF I CAN HEAR, AND BEAUTIFUL MUSIC BEGINS. IT IS CLEAR TO ME THAT I AM IN THE MIND OF GOD; I AM SEEING THE SOURCE OF ALL. AND I KNOW THAT WE ALL EXIST HERE TRULY, AND THIS IS THE LIMITLESS ENERGY THAT GOD OFFERS TO US EVERY MOMENT TO CREATE."

A.D.
ASHEVILLE, NORTH CAROLINA

Grand Unification

This image of a golden diamond came to us with great power and scintillating light. As we meditated on the dazzling radiance we realized that this universal symbol of a diamond is the unity of love. Within the facets of the diamond there exist all of our God virtues and when these virtues come together a beautiful diamond of great value is created.

Meditation on the symbol

Visualize this golden diamond in your mind's eye.

Allow the activation to begin by remembering to relax and put your awareness on your breath.

TAKE SEVERAL DEEP SLOW BREATHS FROM YOUR ABDOMEN.

YOU WILL FEEL THE BLESSING FLOW FROM ABOVE YOUR PHYSICAL BODY, COMING DOWN FROM THE HEAVENS THROUGH YOUR OVER-SOUL AND SOUL, DOWN INTO THE TOP OF YOUR HEAD, DOWN THROUGH YOUR BODY AND ANCHORING AT THE BASE OF YOUR SPINE. THE ENERGY SPREADS THROUGHOUT YOUR ENTIRE PHYSICAL BODY INTO YOUR CELLS, ORGANS AND GLANDS.

AS THE LIGHT OF YOUR SOUL FLOWS DOWN FROM THE HEAVENS INTO YOUR PHYSICAL BODY THERE IS AN OPENING TO THE HIGHER DIMENSIONS ABOVE YOUR HEAD.

THE ILLUMINATING LIGHT FROM GOD POURS THROUGH YOU AND GRACES YOU WITH SO MANY BLESSINGS.

THIS DIVINE LIGHT POURS INTO YOUR PHYSICAL BODY, MENTAL BODY, EMOTIONAL BODY AND ETHERIC BODY.

THE LIGHT OF GOD CONTINUES TO ANCHOR INTO YOU AT THE BASE OF YOUR SPINE, AND DOWN INTO THE EARTH.

WE SUGGEST YOU MEDITATE ON A SYMBOL DAILY FOR 10-15 MINUTES. VISUALIZE THE SYMBOL AND THEN RELAX AND ALLOW THE ACTIVATIONS AND BLESSINGS TO FLOW THROUGH YOU.

Grand Unification

This symbol of the Golden Diamond unites the other 19 sacred symbols that you have received through reading this book and accepting the blessings, activations and initiations.

The journey that a diamond has taken to emerge radiant in its present form, began millions of years ago as carbon. We are reminded of our own journeys and how we have been like the diamond so powerfully transformed into our beauty by this vast and boundless cosmos.

There is a light diamond that exists within you in a non-physical higher dimension. this illuminated radiant diamond contains your perfection.

This Initiation allows for your perfect Diamond to shine forth from within you, out into the world.

By embodying this truth and meditating on your inner golden diamond, you will come to know the depths of your soul and who and what you are.

Your purpose will be revealed to you through your inner-most wisdom. With these blessings you will fulfill your divine plan and purpose to complete your human journey, becoming fully divine.

The more you utilize this blessing, the more real and powerful it becomes to you.

Testimonial

"THE GOLDEN DIAMOND EFFORTLESSLY APPEARS IN MY MIND'S EYE. IT IMMEDIATELY EXPANDS TO SURROUND ME, AND SIMULTANEOUSLY I SEE IT IN MY HEART. I AM FILLED WITH A VIBRATION OF LOVE, PEACE AND I FEEL ONENESS WITH ALL OF CREATION. I FEEL DISSOLVED IN GOD."

BARRY NADLER
ASHEVILLE, NORTH CAROLINA

Christ Consciousness

The golden lotus is a symbol of beauty, prosperity and purity.

The Upanishads contain many references to the lotus in the heart. The lotus within our hearts is where God dwells.

Christ Consciousness is the perfection of the union of human nature and divine consciousness. When our heart and personality are purified, we become anointed and we reflect the light of the Christ.

Meditation on the Symbol

Visualize this golden lotus at the top of your head, in your crown chakra.

Allow the activation to begin by remembering to relax and put your awareness on your breath.

Take several deep slow breaths from your abdomen.

You will feel the blessing flow from above your physical body, coming down from the heavens through your Over-Soul and Soul, down into the top of your head, down through your body and anchoring at the base of your spine. The energy spreads throughout your entire physical body into your cells, organs and glands.

As the light of your Soul flows down from the heavens into your physical body there is an opening to the higher dimensions above your head.

The illuminating light from God pours through you and graces you with so many blessings.

This divine light pours into your physical body, mental body, emotional body and etheric body.

The light of god continues to anchor into you at the base of your spine, and down into the earth.

We suggest you meditate on a symbol daily for 10-15 minutes per day. Visualize the symbol and then relax and allow the activations and blessings to flow through you.

CHRIST CONSCIOUSNESS

IN THE BEGINNING INSTRUCTION SECTION OF OUR BOOK, THE READER WAS GIVEN A MEDITATION TO DO WITH EACH SACRED SYMBOL. THIS MEDITATION CREATES A PERMANENT BRIDGE FROM THE PHYSICAL BODY TO THE HIGHER DIVINE DIMENSIONS AND YOUR ENLIGHTENED MIND.

THIS PERMANENT BRIDGE ALLOWS THE FLOW OF THE HIGHER DIMENSIONS INTO YOUR LOWER BODIES, AND IN THIS PROCESS YOUR LOWER BODIES BECOME PURIFIED AND EVENTUALLY EMANATE THE CHRIST PRESENCE.

THE PRESENCE OF THE CHRIST IS ALIVE IN EVERYBODY ON OUR DEAR PLANET. IN OTHER CULTURES THE CHRIST CONSCIOUSNESS MAY BE REFERRED TO AS THE BUDDHA CONSCIOUSNESS OR ASCENDED CONSCIOUSNESS.

BECOMING ONE IN CONSCIOUSNESS WITH THE HIGHER DIVINE DIMENSIONS, AND ESTABLISHING THE BRIDGE OF LIGHT PERMANENTLY CONNECTING THESE DIMENSIONS OF THE UNIVERSAL MIND OF GOD TO YOUR PHYSICAL BODY, YOU BRIDGE HEAVEN AND EARTH SIMULTANEOUSLY.

YOU LIVE IN THE FLOW OF YOUR SOUL, A HIGHER VIBRATION, ONE WITH THE INFINITE SOURCE OF ALL LIFE. THIS IS CHRIST CONSCIOUSNESS.

TESTIMONIAL

"AS I MEDITATE ON THE SACRED SYMBOL OF THE GOLDEN LOTUS I SEE THE LOTUS IN FRONT OF ME, THEN THE GOLDEN LOTUS MOVES TO THE TOP OF MY HEAD. THIS IS THE CROWNING GLORY FOR THE CONNECTION OF HEAVEN AND EARTH. I AM SO THANKFUL."

MARY NADLER
ASHEVILLE, NORTH CAROLINA

About the Authors

Mary is a great blesser of life being called to serve life with love from a universal level of consciousness. Mary has been blessed with many transformational gifts and will share these gifts with you through her blessings. Mary conducts all the offerings posted on our website.

Barry brings practical mysticism to everyday life, as a reflection of his beautiful heart in action. Barry takes care of his family as a Senior Project Manager who celebrates "chopping wood and carrying water." As a musician, he is also producing several transformational CDs that reflect the higher dimensions of consciousness and the wholeness of being divine.

Becoming teachers

We offer classes to anyone that feels inspired to initiate others into the extraordinary blessings of the sacred symbols contained in this book.

In the Training Classes Level One and Teacher Classes Level Two we will discover the depths of wisdom that these sacred symbols have to share with us.

Offerings

Join our mailing list to receive our monthly newsletter. We facilitate numerous offerings, including a free monthly prayer group called "Circle of Love", a free monthly Full Moon Meditation, retreats, private sessions and seminars.

See our website **www.MaryandBarry.com** for more information.